EX LIBRIS

_____

_____

SACRED
FLOWERS

SACRED FLOWERS

Creating a Heavenly Garden

RONI JAY

BEYOND
WORDS
Publishing
I N C

BEYOND WORDS PUBLISHING, INC.
20827 N.W. Cornell Rd. Suite 500
Hillsboro, Oregon 97124
503-531-8700
1-800-284-9673

© Godsfield Press 1997

Designed and Produced by
THE BRIDGEWATER BOOK COMPANY LTD

Picture Research by Vanessa Fletcher

The publishers wish to thank the following for the use of pictures:
Bridgeman Art Library, e.t. archive

The information contained in this book is intended to be educational
and not for diagnosis, prescription, or treatment of any health disorder whatsoever.
This information should not replace competent medical care.
The editor and publishers are in no way liable for any misuse of the material.
Plants such as the opium poppy are illegal to grow and possess in certain countries.
Refer/confer with your local authorities to be in compliance with all applicable regulations.

First published in Great Britain in 1997 by Godsfield Press

Library of Congress Catalog Card Number 96-80240

ISBN 1–885223–54–4

Printed in Singapore
Distributed to the book trade by Publishers Group West

For a free catalog of other titles by Beyond Words Publishing, Inc.,
please write to us at the address above or call our toll-free number, 1-800-284-9673

The corporate mission of Beyond Words Publishing, Inc.:
Inspire to Integrity

Frontispiece: Indian Man by Abu'l Hasan, 1589

CONTENTS

INTRODUCTION

I f you have ever breathed in the scent of lilies, watched a rose flower open, or looked closely at the seed head of a poppy, you know there is magic in flowers. And the ancients knew it too. For thousands of years people have recognized the spiritual importance of flowers.

Flowers are universally seen as a gift from heaven. But certain flowers in particular are considered sacred, such as the lotus in Asia; the rose, which symbolizes the blood of Christ; and vervain, revered by the Celts. These flowers have a deep spiritual significance to the people who hold them sacred, and they have much to teach us too.

Sacred Flowers is a guide to many of the flowers that are held in great esteem in various cultures around the world. Each of these flowers has something to tell us, and each still has a practical use in the modern world; perhaps we need them more now than ever before. You will find advice here on how to use each flower to expand your mind, soothe your spirit, or heal your body. Some of the flowers have been known to help on several levels – physical, emotional, and spiritual.

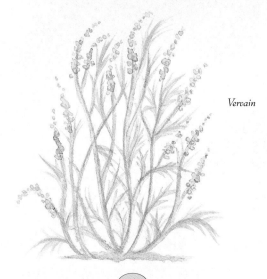

Vervain

USING THE FLOWERS

The flowers included in this book can be used in a number of ways. Many of them can inspire and uplift if you simply look at them or breathe in their scent. If you have a garden, or even just a balcony or a windowsill, you will find that many of the flowers are easy to grow. This is a very rewarding way to experience both the life force and the transience of individual flowers and to watch firsthand their life cycle, which is an integral part of their spiritual significance. For many cultures, flowers represent the cycle of life, death, and rebirth.

Essential oils and teas are two other forms in which you can use flowers. Many essential oils can be bought over the counter. You can burn these oils, add them to your bath water, or incorporate them into massage oils. This will release the scent of the flower to help soothe the emotions, expand the spirit, and sharpen your focus when meditating.

Many of these flowers can also be used to make teas. This method is generally applied when you are using the flower for

Poppy

healing. Be careful to use only those plants that are specifically recommended for teas, since some of the others may do you more harm than good.

Sacred Flowers looks at the ways people have recognized the spiritual, emotional, and physical benefits of flowers throughout the ages. It is also a practical guide to help you tap into this traditional knowledge and to use it to uplift and inspire. You have probably always known, if only unconsciously, that flowers have many sacred and magical properties. This book will help you to learn exactly what those properties are and how they can be put to beneficial use.

LADY'S MANTLE

LATIN NAME *Alchemilla vulgaris*
OTHER NAMES *Lion's foot, bear's foot, dewcup*
MEANING *Feminine principle*

This plant has exceptionally beautiful leaves that are pleated and covered with fine, silky hairs. These resemble an old-fashioned cloak, which is why the plant is commonly known as lady's mantle. Each leaf is thought to resemble the foot of a lion or a bear. If you look at the plant early in the morning, or after a rain, you will find that water has collected in the base of the leaf in little silver droplets. The first part of this flower's Latin name derives from the fact that alchemists used to collect the dew from these leaves each morning to use in experiments that called for water.

Lady's mantle is sacred to the Virgin Mary, who may be the Lady referred to in its name. It was adopted as Mary's flower by the early Christian church because its healing properties were especially important for women. It is sometimes nicknamed "a woman's best friend."

You can make a tea from the fresh or dried leaves and stems, which has been known to relieve numerous gynecological problems. One modern herbalist believes that if all women took lady's mantle tea regularly, gynecological operations would be cut by a third. The most common applications for this plant are to reduce heavy periods, regulate the menstrual cycle, and ease the unpleasant symptoms of menopause, and woman often drink one or two cups of the tea each day until the problem has disappeared.

In the seventeenth century, the herbalist Nicholas Culpeper recommended that women drink two cups of lady's mantle tea every day during pregnancy. It is also drunk for ten days after childbirth, since it helps the womb to contract.

Lady's mantle is a powerful feminine flower. If a woman feels her femininity threatened in any way, it is a good idea to bring a vase of the flowers into the house or to drink tea made from the leaves until her feminine spirit is strengthened or the threat has passed.

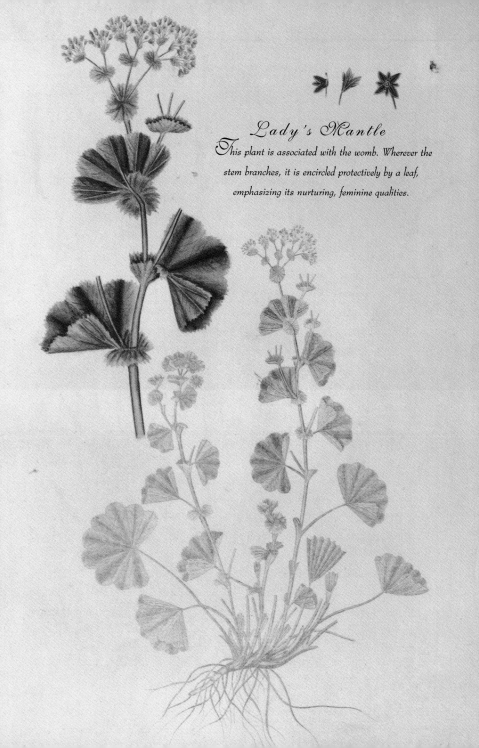

Lady's Mantle

This plant is associated with the womb. Wherever the stem branches, it is encircled protectively by a leaf, emphasizing its nurturing, feminine qualities.

BELLADONNA

LATIN NAME *Atropa belladonna*
OTHER NAMES *Deadly nightshade, witch's berry*
MEANING *Death, beauty*

The Latin name for deadly nightshade, atropa belladonna, reveals its two meanings. The first part of it comes from Atropos, one of the ancient Greek Fates responsible for determining when each mortal would die. The Latin word *belladonna* means "beautiful woman"; women used to dilute the juice of the plant in water and then place drops of the solution in their eyes to dilate their pupils and make themselves more beautiful.

Belladonna has long been associated with dark spirits. The Sumerians used it five thousand years ago to treat people who were possessed by demons. The Greeks used it in much the same way they used mandrake, another of their sacred plants. The maenads – the women who worshiped the god Dionysus – used to add drops of deadly nightshade juice to their wine before their orgies. These orgies became extremely depraved and often led to murder as the women set upon the male followers of Dionysus and tore them apart in their frenzy.

Belladonna has ancient associations with beauty and erotic love. The Greeks added small quantities of the plant sap to their wine as an aphrodisiac, and European witches incorporated it into love potions. Deadly nightshade is one of the most important of the witches' plants. In the middle ages it was a standard ingredient in love spells and in flying ointments as well as in any charms and amulets with a darker purpose.

It is extremely dangerous to take belladonna in any quantity or to eat the berries, which are unfortunately very appealing to children. However, you can put a piece of the dried root, wrapped in a silk scarf or placed in a silk purse, under your mattress beneath the head of your bed if you fear that your partner is straying. If you focus on it as you fall asleep, your partner, too, may become refocused on the relationship and abandon any thoughts of wandering. (You may also find that it gives you erotic dreams.)

Belladonna

Belladonna has always been both valued and feared. Heavily diluted, it has been known to ease many ills, but in stronger concentrations it can kill. To Germans of the past it was the fruit of the Valkyries and was associated with Valhalla and the afterlife.

DAISY

LATIN NAME *Bellis perennis*
OTHER NAMES *Bruisewort, baby's pet*
MEANING *Innocence*

The common lawn daisy can also grow in a double form that is sometimes pink or red. Its name means "day's eye," because it closes up its petals at night. This flower belongs to the sun. There is nothing dark or secretive about the honest daisy — it is a flower of the light.

As well as symbolizing innocence, the daisy is also the flower of children, who love to pick the flowers and make daisy chains from them. The daisy chain — which should always be joined at the ends to form a circle with no discernible starting point — represents the sun and the totality of the world that it sustains. It is also a protective charm; the Irish have long believed that a daisy chain protects the child who wears it from being carried away by fairies. Picked daisies, either pinned to the clothing or brought indoors and placed in a vase, will also act as a protection against external threats.

The daisy is a healing plant; the leaves can be eaten fresh or infused as a tea that has been known to ease rheumatic aches and pains, general stiffness, and backache. If the crushed leaves are applied to a bruise, they can help to reduce any swelling, which is how the plant earns its common name of "bruisewort."

An old-fashioned form of daisy known as "hens-and-chickens," or the "childling" daisy, was popular in medieval times. This flower sends out up to a dozen tiny stalks from each main flower, and these stalks also have a flower on the end. This plant has always been considered mystical and is especially associated with children since the flowers appear to bear their own children.

The circle of baby flowers around the main flower symbolizes a halo around the sun. For this reason, the leaves of the plants bring special blessings to anyone who eats them. Most favored of all are the children of women who eat these leaves while they are pregnant.

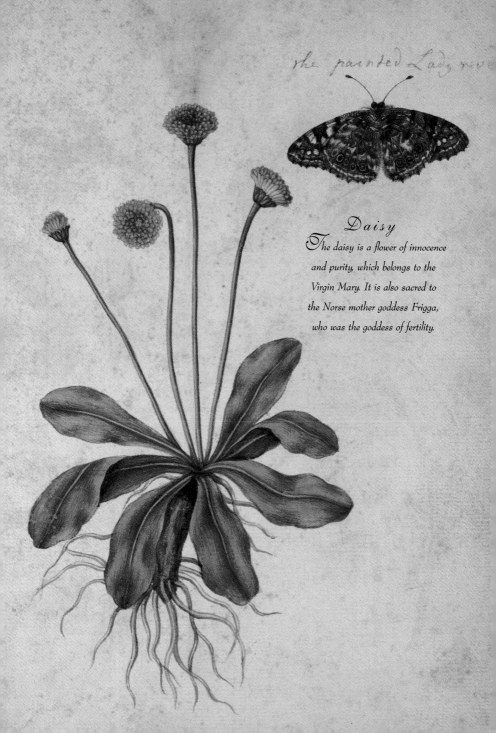

Daisy

The daisy is a flower of innocence
and purity, which belongs to the
Virgin Mary. It is also sacred to
the Norse mother goddess Frigga,
who was the goddess of fertility.

CHRYSANTHEMUM

LATIN NAME *Chrysanthemum morifolium*
OTHER NAME *None*
MEANING *Longevity, contemplation*

This plant, which takes its name from the Greek for "golden flower," has long been sacred in the East. In Japan it is the national flower and the ancient symbol of the mikado, or emperor, bestowing long life on him.

According to legend, the emperor had a favorite named Keu Tze Tung, who accidentally offended him and was banished from the court. Keu Tze Tung traveled until he arrived in the Valley of the Chrysanthemum, where a stream flowed through fields carpeted in the flowers. The stream was fed by the dew dropping from the petals of the flowers; when he drank from the stream he became immortal.

In China, the chrysanthemum is a recurring motif in religious art; it is used to decorate temples and sacred texts. The Chinese have a legend similar to that of the Japanese; in this version anyone who drinks from the stream that flows between the flowers will live to be one hundred years old.

The chrysanthemum still has its place in traditional Chinese medicine. A tea made from the dried flowers is drunk to prolong life. It is a flower of contemplation, so the tea is also used to clear the head before a period of prolonged thought or meditation. At one time it was added to church flower arrangements to keep the congregation attentive during the sermon.

Chrysanthemum tea has been known to clear the mind of distractions such as headaches or depression; the Chinese have long used it for this purpose. The Koreans make a tea by boiling the roots, which they use to cure vertigo as well as depression.

The flower tea is a useful remedy for fear of heights – both real and metaphorical. If you are worried that you are climbing too high a mountain in your career, your relationships, or some other part of your life, chrysanthemum tea can clear your mind and steady your nerves so that you may reach the summit of your ambitions with confidence.

Chrysanthemum

The greatest honor you can win in Japan is the Order of the Chrysanthemum.

It is sacred in China too, where its petals are eaten in salads

to increase longevity.

SACRED GARDENS

Any garden is sacred. As a place where nature is ordered, a garden symbolizes the conscious rather than the unconscious. Your senses are heightened and stimulated in a garden, lifting you onto a more conscious plane. You can expand the spirituality of your garden further by your choice of garden layout and the flowers you plant.

SACRED SHAPES

The very simplest sacred design for a garden is one based on the circle. If your boundary is not circular, you can create a circle, or several of them, by the shape of flower beds, grass, or even containers. Indian spiritual gardens often have circular designs, forming a living mandala. You can plant flowers in shapes and colors to create your own mandala. The circle is particularly appropriate to gardens since it represents the wheel of life and the continuous changing of the seasons.

Gardens based on squares represent universal order, earthliness, and security. If you want your garden to be a hideaway somewhere, you can feel safe and sheltered, a layout based on concentric squares, or a square bordered by smaller squares, will help to increase this atmosphere.

The Celtic symbol of the triple enclosure can be adapted as a garden design, perhaps for a herb garden within a larger garden. The inner square symbolizes the human subconscious; the outer square represents the senses as they relate to the outside world; and the middle square is that part of the mind where the senses and the subconscious meet. The whole symbol represents human consciousness.

Mazes and knot gardens, even if you have room for only the simplest version, represent the journey of the spirit through confusion to enlightenment at the center. Place a beautiful ornament or a small pool at the center, and use this spot for meditation.

SACRED PLANTING

When planting your garden, choose sacred flowers, such as the ones in this book. Make plenty of room for the flowers that impart the qualities you most seek, for instance, calmness, protection, or enlightenment. Or create a healing garden of sacred flowers that can be used medicinally.

Another option is to make a meditation garden, perhaps including sacred flowers used for focusing the mind. You might create an astrological garden with twelve sections, perhaps concentrating on the plant that appertains to your own sun sign.

Thyme

SUN SIGNS AND THEIR SACRED FLOWERS

ARIES...*Rosemary*
TAURUS...*Thyme*
GEMINI...*Vervain*
CANCER..*Daisy*
LEO..*Poppy*
VIRGO...*Southernwood*
LIBRA...*Violet*
SCORPIO...*Tarragon*
SAGITTARIUS...*Feverfew*
CAPRICORN...*Solomon's seal*
AQUARIUS..*Elder*
PISCES ....*Rose*

ORANGE BLOSSOM

LATIN NAME *Citrus spp.*
OTHER NAMES *None*
MEANING *Calmness*

The orange tree originally came from central Asia, but when the Arabs found it valuable for trading, it quickly became distributed to both the West and the East. It was so popular that it was not long before orange trees were growing in warm climates from Spain to China. The beneficial properties of orange flowers were soon recognized; their first mention is in early Chinese and Arab herbals.

The orange flower was revered because of its scent, which was so fresh and pure that it could only come from a plant which was itself pure. The orange tree became a symbol of spiritual innocence and freshness, and because of the calming effect of its scent, it was seen to impart a quiet, meditative mind, even to be able to empty the mind in preparation for meditation.

There is a Buddhist story of a young monk who was particularly adept at emptying his mind. One day, as he was sitting under an orange tree, the blossoms began to fall around him. The gods whispered, "We are blessing you because of your words about emptiness." "But I didn't speak," replied the monk. The gods responded, "You did not speak, and we did not hear. That is true emptiness." And they continued to shower him with orange blossoms.

The scent of orange flowers is a sedative, which is why they have long been an ingredient of potpourri and pomanders. Orange flower water has a similar effect and is taken to treat nervous complaints such as those forms of indigestion and insomnia that are caused by stress. One of the most popular ways to take it is by pouring a few drops onto a lump of sugar.

Orange flowers, or orange flower water, is a valuable remedy for stress. The purity and freshness of the flowers help to draw out tensions and strains and leave both the mind and the body relaxed and calm. You can take orange flower water internally or use the scent of the fresh flowers or the oil. It is useful as a permanent calming remedy in the bedroom. If you have trouble sleeping, make sure the room is always scented with orange flowers.

Orange de Malte.

Orange Blossom

The fruit of the orange tree represents the sun because of its color. Like the sun, the orange bestows fertility and good fortune, which is often symbolized in art by depicting the Christ child holding an orange.

THORN APPLE

LATIN NAME *Datura spp.*

OTHER NAMES *Jimson weed, stinkweed, angel's trumpet, devil's apple*

MEANING *Forgetfulness, prophecy*

This powerful and dangerous plant has been revered by many cultures around the world. Native to Central America, India, and Asia, it was introduced to Europe by the Gypsies. Early European settlers brought the plant to North America.

The thorn apple was sacred to the Indian Thug sect, who worshiped the dark goddess Kali. The Thugs used to take thorn apple themselves, and they would also give the juice of the plant to their victims, whom they would then kill as a sacrifice to their goddess.

Thorn apple induces a state of forgetfulness. Those who drink its juice usually remember nothing of what they have done while under its influence. The Algonquian people of North America incorporated thorn apple into their initiation ceremony for boys passing into manhood. It would induce a state of semimadness for about three weeks, after which the boys would begin adulthood with all memories of their childhood erased.

Thorn apple is used medicinally in Central and South America. It is given to people before operations as an anesthetic; sometimes fresh flowers are placed on painful parts of the body to produce a numbing effect. It is still a sacred plant, and rituals surround its collection and its use.

Thorn apple is an aid to both astral projection and prophecy. It is extremely dangerous to ingest any part of the plant, even in relatively low doses. However, you can smell the flowers – which may be mildly narcotic – to help you to do astral projection or to make decisions that require an insight into the future. This is best done in the open air and not in a closed room, since even the scent can be mildly toxic.

Thorn Apple

Thorn apple was associated with witchcraft – the dark feminine art –
when it was introduced to Europe. Witches included the juices of thorn apple
in the ointments they prepared to help them fly.

HELLEBORE

LATIN NAME *Helleborus niger*
OTHER NAMES *Christmas rose, black hellebore, black nisewort*
MEANING *Protection*

Hellebore was associated with demons by the ancient Greeks, who used to administer it to people who were possessed, including the maenads – the women who worshiped Dionysus with drunken orgies. All species of hellebore are toxic, but some more than others. The black hellebore was used by the Gauls to poison the tips of their arrows, and seeds have even been found in prehistoric tombs. We can only guess at the plant's function for these ancient peoples, but the plant must have been sacred or magical to earn a place in their burial chambers.

The black hellebore gets its common name from the color of its root, which is the part most often used for sacred or medicinal purposes. The flowers themselves are white and blossom as early as December, which accounts for its other name, the Christmas rose. The plant's ability to flower so beautifully even in the depths of winter has earned it a reputation for special powers; it is a plant of protection, and if you plant it outside the door to your house it will keep evil spirits away.

Medicinally, hellebore has been used to expel unwanted illnesses or conditions from the body. As well as driving out demons, it has long been used as a cure for worms in children (although too high a dose can be fatal). The leaves, if dried and powdered, induce sneezing, which accounts for another of its common names: black nisewort.

Hellebore has also been used to drive away unexplained feelings of foreboding – that awful feeling that something is terribly wrong but you don't know what. Bring a vase of hellebores into the room with you and let the flowers drive away the unpleasant atmosphere and replace it with one of calm and protection.

A Christmas rose brought into the house for the Christmas festival will bring blessing and protection. Bring it indoors in a pot; if you cut the flowers they will die and so will their special influence.

Helleborus niger,
Orientalis, amplissimo
folio, caule praealto,
flore viridi, Itineris
Tournefort.

Hellebore

Those who dig it up pray to Apollo and Asclepius by observing the eagle's
flight. They say that the bird's flight is dangerous, for it would bring
death if it saw hellebore being dug.

Dioscorides, Greek physician, 1st century A.D.

ST. JOHN'S WORT

LATIN NAME *Hypericum perforatum*

OTHER NAMES *None*

MEANING *The solar principle*

 St. John's wort gets its name from the fact that it flowers on Midsummer's Day, which is also St. John's Day – June 24. Before the Christian calendar was introduced, this was around the same date as the pagan summer solstice festival, which is why St. John's wort is the flower of the sun.

St. John's wort has long been used to drive away evil spirits. This is largely because it belongs to the sun, which no one can hide from, but also because if you crush the leaves they release a smell of incense – a smell associated with religious festivals and rituals.

People possessed by evil spirits were often made to inhale the scent of the leaves, or to drink a tea made from the flowers, to drive out the demons inside them. And it was traditional to hang a branch of the plant above the door on Midsummer's Day to keep witches and evil spirits away. It is wise to carry a sprig of St. John's wort when out walking at night, since no demon will be able to approach you while you are holding this sacred flower.

This flower is a natural healing plant. The yellow flowers are crushed and steeped in oil, sealed in a jar, and left in the sun for two or three weeks. At the end of this time the oil will have turned deep red (the flowers, when crushed, release a red oil). It is used for all sorts of ailments such as cuts, sores, burns, sprains, and skin conditions. It is also an age-old treatment for rheumatism and gout and, taken internally either as an oil or as a tea, for stomach cramps and internal aches and pains.

St. John's wort is also used to ease nervousness and depression. It imparts the warmth, life, and energy of the sun to anyone who uses it externally or internally, and it feeds the soul. Just as feeling the sun on your skin on a warm day gives you a positive feeling and a joy in life, so taking St. John's wort will make you feel happy and confident.

St. John's Wort

*If you hold the leaves of St. John's wort up to the light, you can see the
oil glands in them, which look like spots. This oil is valuable
for treating all sorts of ailments.*

SACRED GARLANDS AND POSIES

Violets

lowers have been collected and displayed in garlands and posies for centuries. Partly this is, of course, decorative. But garlands and posies have a deeper significance as well.

GARLANDS AND WREATHS

The garland or wreath forms a circle with no beginning and no end; this symbolizes eternity and the cycle of life, death, and rebirth. It is made from flowers because these too represent life and death and the changing of the seasons. The garland acts as a link in a chain. It joins this world with the next, which is why wreaths are incorporated into funeral ceremonies. It is also a symbol of friendship because it joins people together. In ancient India and China, garlands were hung over the temple doors on feast days to symbolize the fellowship of the people within.

The garland brings good luck because it is in the shape of a ring, an ancient symbol of fortune. Garlands and wreaths hung on doors to bring protection and good fortune should be made from flowers of friendship and protection, such as elder, myrtle, rosemary, roses, and violets.

POSIES

It was customary in European countries to make up posies of flowers and hang them upside down from the beams to dry so that they would last all year. These posies contained sacred flowers that would bestow their influence in the house or in the particular

Roses

room where they were used. The posy always has one central flower; this is the heart of the posy's influence. Round the central flower should be either six or eight other flowers, creating the sacred numbers seven or nine.

For a posy that will bring a general blessing on the house, collect the flowers on Midsummer's Day, June 24, since this is the height of summer when the plants have drunk as much of the sun's energy as they will all year. At the center of the posy you should place the sun's flower, St. John's wort.

To purify the house at the winter solstice, following an ancient pagan tradition, collect the flowers on August 14. Place lavender at the center, surrounded by eight fragrant, evergreen plants such as rosemary, thyme, southernwood, myrtle, sage, pinks, bay, and juniper. Hang the posy to dry and at the solstice take it down and burn it in a pan, carrying it through the house to distribute the incenselike, purifying smoke.

Lavender, Rosemary, Sage, Pinks, Bay, Thyme

MORNING GLORY

LATIN NAME *Ipomoea violacea*

OTHER NAMES *Tlitliltzin*

MEANING *Death and rebirth*

This flower, which is now commonly grown as a garden plant in Europe, is native to the Americas. It grows in Mexico and was sacred to the Aztecs. It has beautiful blue saucer-shaped flowers, each of which opens in the morning and dies the same evening, which is why morning glory symbolizes death and rebirth.

The seeds of morning glory are hallucinogenic, and the Aztecs used to make an infusion of them and drink it. This created a trance state in which they communicated with spirits from the world of the dead. Mexican healers still use this technique to help them learn more about the illness of the person they are healing.

The Aztec priests used the seeds of morning glory, mixed with tobacco and insects, to rub on their bodies before performing sacrifices. The Aztec word for morning glory seeds was *tlitliltzin*, which means "sacred black." The Aztecs preferred to use willing sacrificial victims, and the morning glory seeds would guarantee the victims that after passing through death they would then be reborn. We too can use the morning glory to help us pass from one phase of life to another, a symbolic death and rebirth. For example, you may be changing jobs or moving on from a relationship that has died.

Be warned, however, that commercial morning glory seeds are coated with a poison, and even untreated seeds can be dangerous, especially during pregnancy, when they may cause an abortion. Midwives in parts of Central and South America give morning glory seeds to ease labor and birth; since we are in a constant cycle of death and life, every birth is also a rebirth.

You can grow morning glories very easily in a pot in a sunny spot on a windowsill or balcony if you don't have a garden. Each morning, look at the crumpled petals of yesterday's flowers and then at the new flowers opening. This will help you to meditate and reflect on the natural cycle of change to the next stage of your own life.

Morning Glory

Morning glory plants still grow in many parts of Mexico which were once ancient ritual sites of the Aztecs, or other places of power.

LILY

LATIN NAME *Lilium candidum*

OTHER NAMES *White lily, Madonna lily*

MEANING *Purity*

The lily has possibly been in cultivation longer than any other flower. Its image has been found decorating three- thousand-year-old pottery from Crete. It was cultivated throughout the ancient Mediterranean world, though largely as a food plant since the bulbs are edible. But it was considered so valuable that the Greeks and Romans held it sacred to their mother goddesses, Hera and Juno.

The very first lily is said to have grown in the Garden of Eden from the tears dropped by Eve when she was driven out. The white lily is the emblem of the Virgin Mary because when she ascended to heaven her tomb was empty except for lilies and roses. The lily was consecrated to her by the Christian church in the second century A.D., although it did not acquire its common name, the Madonna lily, until about a hundred years ago. The whiteness of the flower symbolizes the Madonna's purity; the gold anthers represent her soul in heaven.

The lily is a common theme in Christian religious painting; when depicted standing in a vase, it symbolizes the feminine principle. Lilies are often included in wedding bouquets because they belong to the Virgin Mary. By the same token, they are used at many other religious festivals, including funerals, so lilies are sometimes associated with death.

Lilies were traditionally grown near fields of wheat; the wheat nourishes the body from within while the lily heals its outer wounds. Its crushed petals are used as a remedy for burns, stings, and cuts, and the bulb – cooked and mixed with milk and flour – is used as a poultice for chilblains, abscesses, and numerous other skin ailments. Lilies growing near wheat also acted as an indicator of the price the grain would fetch. The more flowers on each stem of the lily, the better price the wheat will fetch when it is harvested.

Lily

Thy navel is like a round goblet, which wanteth not liquor:

thy belly is like a heap of wheat set about with lilies.

Song of Solomon 7:2

MYRTLE

LATIN NAME *Myrtus communis*
OTHER NAMES *None*
MEANING *Love*

Grow a myrtle bush on either side of your door, and they will bring love and peace to the household. Myrtle has always been a flower of love, ever since it was the sacred flower of the goddess Aphrodite, or Venus. She was born naked from the waves, and when she first emerged from the sea she hid herself under a myrtle bush. From then on she wore a wreath of myrtle, and the bush was planted around the temples that were dedicated to her worship.

The myrtle is an evergreen plant, and it will keep any love everlasting. The Greeks and the Romans would drink myrtle tea to preserve love; often lovers would drink the tea together to keep their love strong. There is a Persian story that Adam brought Eve a sprig of myrtle after they were banished from paradise. Since biblical times the plant has traditionally been worn or carried by the bride at weddings to bestow lasting love on the newlywed couple.

Myrtle is associated with chastity, which is why it is worn by brides-to-be. For the same reason, it also used to be worn by young girls attending their first Holy Communion. Since it represents the virginal, pure love of the young, it is a children's flower.

Love and beauty go together, and for hundreds of years myrtle flowers and leaves, crushed and steeped in oil, have been used to keep the skin fresh and youthful. The tea has also been used to help retain youth and beauty.

Myrtle leaves and stems are wonderfully fragrant when crushed, and the flowers, too, are sweetly scented. The smell of either of these helps to instill a feeling of well-being and to lift any heaviness of heart or unhappiness. If your spirits need lifting, burn a few drops of myrtle oil or add them to your bath. It is a particularly good scent to use for children; if they are unhappy, add the oil to their bathwater or place a sprig of fresh myrtle under a baby's mattress.

Myrtus Pimenta.

Myrtle

Myrtle is sometimes known as the flower of the gods. If you dream about it,
it signifies good fortune and long life. If you have room to grow only a few plants,
make myrtle one of them.

NARCISSUS

LATIN NAME *Narcissus spp.*
OTHER NAMES *Daffodil, jonquil*
(both are types of narcissus), daffodilly, lent lily
MEANING *Numbness, new beginnings*

The word *narcissus* comes from the Greek *narkao*, meaning "to numb"; the scent of the flowers in an enclosed space can be strong enough to induce a headache and sometimes, according to the Greeks, to cause lethargy. In extreme cases, so they said, it could even cause madness and death. Consequently they associated it with death. According to Greek mythology, Narcissus was a young man who fell so in love with himself when he saw his reflection in a pool that he drowned trying to reach his own image. On his death, his body was transformed into the flower known as narcissus.

The Greeks were not the only people to associate the narcissus with death. The ancient Egyptians also viewed the jonquil as a flower of the underworld because of its scent and wove it into their funeral wreaths; fragments still survive today from thousands of years ago. In medieval Europe it was believed that if a daffodil drooped as you were looking at it, it was an omen of death.

The Arabians, however, viewed the scent as an aphrodisiac, and for the Indians it is one of the sacred oils they rub on their skin before entering the temple to pray. Narcissus oil is used in other parts of the world to treat complaints such as epilepsy and hysteria. The fragrance is hypnotic and focuses the mind when a calming influence is needed. Narcissus oil is a wonderful aromatherapy cure for an agitated mind.

The daffodil is also the flower of new beginnings because it heralds the start of spring. It is the national flower of Wales because it blooms on March 1, the feast day of the patron saint of Wales, St. David. The day you see the first daffodil open is a propitious day to start new projects or to make new resolutions. If you want to strike out in a new direction in your life but find you have difficulty getting started, try burning a little narcissus oil and focusing your mind on how to take that first step; the rest should follow easily.

Narcissus

To the Chinese, the narcissus is an especially propitious flower because it opens
at their new year. They see it as a herald of good fortune.

SACRED FLOWERS IN DREAMS

o dream of flowers is usually very lucky. Flowers symbolize good things, so picking them in a dream indicates that you are gathering good luck and prosperity for your future. If someone else gives flowers to you, this indicates that the person wishes you well.

However, if the flowers in your dream are dead or dying, this is a warning that you must focus on the important things in your life; do not allow yourself to drift or your luck will leave you. If you scatter a bouquet of flowers in your dream, it is a message that you are wasting opportunities in your life.

The color of the flowers you dream of can also be a clue to the message they carry. Red flowers symbolize friendship and love, while white flowers represent death – not of a person but of a phase or situation in your life. If you dream of white flowers, do not ignore the dream when you wake, but focus on it and try to understand what it is telling you. Your dream may be letting you know that a certain friendship has run its course or that now is a good time to change your job.

Certain flowers have specific meanings if they appear in your dreams; your unconscious is using them to relay messages to your conscious mind.

LILY

The lily, a flower of purity, relates to your career. Your prospects are excellent, but you must work hard and avoid corruption if you want to realize them.

NARCISSUS

Outdoors, this flower is a sign of promising new beginnings. But if you dream of narcissus indoors, it suggests some kind of betrayal or guilt on your part. Consider carefully if your dream is telling you that it is better to confess and get the issue out in the open.

ROSE

This flower of love tells you that a friendship is strong and healthy. If someone hands you a rose in a dream, it is a sign that you can trust them.

SNOWDROP

This is a discreet flower, and it symbolizes secrets. To dream of a snowdrop indicates that you are hiding something or keeping a secret that it would be better to share.

Narcissus

LOTUS

LATIN NAME *Nelumbo nucifera*
OTHER NAMES *None*
MEANING *Enlightenment*

The lotus grows like a water lily: its roots are in the mud, the stem grows up through the water, and the heavily scented flower lies above the water, in the sunlight. This pattern of growth symbolizes the progress of the soul from the primeval mud of materialism, through the waters of experience, and into the bright sunshine of enlightenment.

For this reason, the lotus was the most sacred of plants in all Asian and Oriental cultures. The Hindus depict the lotus growing from the navel of Vishnu and show the whole universe emanating from the sun at its center. It also symbolizes the feminine aspect, and it is therefore the flower of love. The Chinese, too, eat the roots and seeds as a love potion.

The lotus is depicted with varying numbers of petals. These circular designs are used as mandalas – sacred abstract pictures that represent the universe and can be used to meditate on the path toward enlightenment.

The lotus was also sacred to the Egyptians, although their sacred lotus was actually a different plant, the blue water lily. Like the lotus of the East, it too symbolized love. The Egyptians cultivated the blue lotus in their gardens and regarded it as the first flower, which opened to reveal the sun at the beginning of creation.

The blue lotus was associated with the Egyptian sun god Ra, because its petals open in the morning and close at night. It symbolized rebirth for the same reason: each morning it opens afresh.

Concentrate on the lotus mandala when meditating; without the love it represents you can never achieve enlightenment. Look deep into its heart and find the center and origin of all creation. Remember where its roots are and use this to remind yourself that enlightenment can be achieved from the muddiest of beginnings; it is the route you take and the goal you reach that matter, not where you started from.

Lotus

I am this pure lotus which went forth from the sunshine,

which is at the nose of Ra. I have descended that I may seek it for Horus,

for I am the pure one who issued from the fen.

Egyptian Book of the Dead, Chapter 81

OPIUM POPPY

LATIN NAME *Papaver somniferum*
OTHER NAMES *Lettuce-leaf poppy*
MEANING *Sexual pleasure*

The opium poppy has been cultivated for thousands of years for its narcotic and medicinal properties. The unripe seed pods are the source of opium, which was often dissolved in alcohol to create laudanum; and morphine is derived from it as well; both opium and laudanum have been taken for medicinal purposes. Opium is a strong painkiller and was used as a cure-all among the Assyrians over two and a half thousand years ago. The Egyptians, Greeks, and Indians also used it as a universal remedy, as did physicians of the Middle Ages, and it is still used in medicines to this day.

Roman legend tells how Somnus, the god of sleep (whose Greek counterpart was Hypnos), created the poppy to send the goddess Ceres to sleep. Ceres was the goddess of the harvest, and she was so exhausted that it was making the wheat crops fail. After her long sleep, she woke revived and the wheat also revived and grew again.

The Arabs valued opium as an inebriant, and some Sufis used it to bring on a mystical trance. The Arabs almost certainly introduced the opium poppy to China and the Far East, and shamans of Northeast Asia used it to induce a trance that would help them travel into the world of spirits.

The Chinese also associated opium with sexuality, for which it became an important symbol. They sold it molded into the shape of a fish, their symbol of good fortune, and recommended it as an aphrodisiac. Many practitioners of Tantric and Taoist love techniques, who use sex as a means of attaining greater spirituality, would take these aphrodisiacs before making love. Opium was also used as an aphrodisiac in India and was consecrated to the god Shiva.

Dried poppy seeds do not contain any opium at all, but they are a symbol of sexual love and contain some relaxing and aphrodisiac properties. They have also been used as part of the regular diet by persons who suffer from nervous tension.

Opium Poppy

Opium induces a sleepy, trance-like state, which is where the flower earns
its Latin name somniferum, meaning "sleep-inducing." Among other things,
the poppy symbolizes the final sleep of death.

PASSION FLOWER

LATIN NAME *Passiflora caerulea*
OTHER NAMES *None*
MEANING *Christian faith, suffering*

The passion flower was named by the Spanish priests who saw it in its native South America. It symbolizes the passion, or crucifixion, of Christ and was therefore sacred to the Catholics when it was first introduced into Europe.

The passion flower has a corona, or crown, of spindly filaments inside the petals, which represents the crown of thorns. The five sepals symbolize the five wounds Christ suffered on the cross. The long style, split into three at the end, shows the three nails used to nail Christ to the cross – one for each hand and one for the feet. The circle of darker markings in the center of the flower represents the halo around Christ's head.

The passion flower is a climbing plant that clings to whatever it grows up with long curling tendrils. This symbolizes Christ holding firm to his purpose, supported by the love of God. It shows how we too will find the strength to suffer if we have the support of our God, which we can earn through faith.

The passion flower is a powerful plant to focus on during times of suffering or anytime we feel our faith in life or our faith in God begin to fail. At the end of the suffering we will see our faith bear fruit, just as the passion flower itself bears a rich, sweet, golden-colored fruit.

Times of doubt are generally times of worry. The passion flower is also a traditional cure for insomnia caused by worry and nerves; it has the power to bring on a restful sleep, and you will wake the next morning feeling refreshed and ready to face the day. You can take the homeopathic remedy Passiflora or make a mild tea from the dried flowers and leaves of the plant.

PASSION FLOWER TEA

Drop about 1 ounce of dried passion flowers and leaves into 2 cups of water. Heat slowly and allow to boil for about a minute. Turn off the heat and let it infuse for ten minutes. Strain the tea before drinking it.

Passion Flower

This flower was often depicted in church stained-glass windows

because of its strong Christian symbolism representing

God summoning converts to His church.

ROSE

LATIN NAME *Rosa spp.*
OTHER NAMES *None*
MEANING *Love*

Both the red and white roses are sacred to the Virgin Mary in Christian teaching; the white signifies her purity, and the red represents the blood of Christ. The word *rosary* comes from the Latin for "rose garden."

The five-petalled wild rose is associated with Christ on earth because it forms the human shape with arms spread out and legs apart, which fits into a five-pointed star. It therefore represents divine love in its earthly form. It also incorporates both the love of Christ, in the symbolism of its flower, and His suffering, in its thorns.

The rose is an important sacred flower around the world because of its beauty and its scent. The Muslims believe that the rose was created from the sweat of Mohammed. The ancient Egyptians held it sacred, and roses have been found buried in Egyptian tombs. Both the Greeks and the Romans revered the rose; the Romans used roses at weddings and funerals, and as a hangover cure. The Hindus oil themselves with rose oil, along with other oils, in preparation for prayer and worship. The Persians believed that the nightingale sings mournfully every time it sees a rose picked; it loves the rose so much that it cannot bear to see it hurt.

The oldest known variety of rose is the Apothecary's rose (*Rosa gallica officinalis*), traditionally used – as oil or attar of roses, or as dried petals – to heal the heart and to create a feeling of happiness. It is almost impossible to smell a rose without feeling your spirits lift. You can use rose petals, perhaps in a potpourri, or rose oil to help woo the one you love. You will be in good company: Cleopatra seduced Antony in a room that was knee-deep in rose petals.

You can also use rose water to purify a place that is tainted in some way. The Muslim conqueror Saladin ordered his followers to wash the Omar mosque in rose water when he finally entered Jerusalem.

Rose

In the thirteenth century, church architecture first incorporated the rose window,
a round stained-glass window whose intricate design was based on the rose,
much as Eastern mandalas have been based on the lotus.

SACRED FLOWER RITUALS

When using a sacred flower to help you on a physical, mental, emotional, or spiritual level, you will maximize its effect if you encompass certain rituals. The flower will still give you its beneficial influence without these rituals, but following these suggestions will enhance the effect and sharpen your own focus and concentration.

HARVESTING

If possible, it is better to pick the flowers yourself. Make sure that you are relaxed when you do this; do not harvest the plants when in a hurry or when your mind is elsewhere. It is better to pick flowers in the morning, when their essence is at its strongest.

Before you take the parts of the plant that you need, pause for a moment and look at the whole plant and appreciate its form, its color, and its scent. Then ask its permission to take the parts you need, explaining why you want them. After you have picked what you need, thank the plant for giving you part of itself.

PREPARING

Always treat the harvested parts of the plant with respect. Do not dump them on the kitchen table while you do something else; if you are not going to use them immediately, put them carefully in water. Whatever you are doing with the plant – infusing it, drying it, or anything else – handle it with care. And while you are preparing it, think about the effect you want it to have when the preparations are complete.

USING

Again, keep your mind focused on the sacred use to which you are putting the flower. Do not hurriedly drink a cup of tea made from the flower while you are on your way out of the door. Sit down and concentrate on what you are using it for.

If you are going to put the flowers in a vase, or wrap part of the plant in silk, or burn the essential oil while you meditate, it will help to choose an appropriate color for the vase, the silk, or the candle that heats the oil. Different colors are suitable for bringing about different effects. Choose the color that seems most apt; where two or more colors seem suitable, make an intuitive choice as to which you prefer.

RED .... *passion, sexual desire, warming*
ORANGE .... *freedom, independence*
YELLOW .... *cheerfulness*
GREEN .... *balance, judgment, self-control*
PALE BLUE .... *calmness, relaxation*
BLUE .... *abstinence, conscientiousness*
PURPLE .... *spirituality, purification, mysticism*
PINK .... *creativity*
BROWN .... *stability, security*
BLACK .... *the unconscious*
WHITE .... *purity, enlightenment*
GOLD .... *self-confidence*

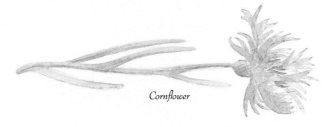

Cornflower

ROSEMARY

LATIN NAME *Rosmarinus officinalis*
OTHER NAMES *None*
MEANING *Friendship*

The first known use of rosemary was by the ancient Egyptians, who used to burn it as a cleansing incense, a popular use ever since. The old French name for the plant was *insensier*. It has been burned at funerals and in hospitals and used as incense in church. It was also recommended that rosemary be inhaled to protect against colds and "weakness of the brain":

> "Against weakness of the brain and coldness thereof, set rosemary in wine and let the patient receive the smoke at his nose and keep his head warm." (*The Grete Herball*, 1526)

Rosemary has long been associated with remembrance, generally in the sense of faithfulness and friendship (although in ancient Greece, pupils used to wear it in their hair during exams). In Asia, people used to plant it on graves in the hope that their ancestors would remember the bond between them and continue to give help and guidance after death.

The rosemary bush is sacred in Christian lore because the Virgin Mary is said to have taken shelter under a rosemary bush on the flight to Egypt. She spread her blue cloak over the bush to dry, and the flowers, previously white, turned blue.

Rosemary is a very useful healing herb for headaches, dizziness, mental tiredness, and other problems of the head. Try burning the leaves and branches, or the oil, to release the restorative, aromatic scent of the plant. If your mind is cluttered and you want to restore its clarity, massage the oil into the temples.

The fresh stems, in flower if possible, will help to restore an ailing friendship. Cut several stems from the same plant, keep some for yourself, and give the rest to the person whose friendship you want to preserve. Or cook your friend a meal that includes rosemary; as you prepare the food, concentrate on the other person and the aspects of the friendship you want to maintain.

Rosemary

Lovers have exchanged sprigs of rosemary for thousands of years
as a sign of faithfulness, and it is carried at weddings, funerals, and other ceremonies
that remember friendship or ask for solemn vows to be sworn.

ELDER

LATIN NAME *Sambucus nigra*
OTHER NAMES *Black elder, European elder*
MEANING *Compassion*

The elder tree has been sacred among the peoples of western Europe since the time of the Celts. It is loved for its many healing powers – every part of the plant has been used to treat some ailment or condition – but it is also held in awe because of its association with witches. The elder tree was the tree from which Judas Iscariot hanged himself, which is why witches have adopted it.

It is unlucky to harm an elder tree, because it is the witch's ally. You should never cut its branches, bring them into the house, or burn them. If you fall asleep under an elder tree, the smell is believed to cause you to sleep so deeply you may never wake up.

However, you can live in harmony with the elder tree as long as you always ask its permission before you take any part of it. A traditional chant to recite as you cut the flowers, leaves, or bark goes like this:

Old woman, old woman,
Give me your wood,
And when I am dead,
I'll give you mine.

Some say that as long as you treat the elder with respect, it will protect you from witches and evil spirits. An elder tree outside the back door will protect the house. It is best if the tree has put itself there, but if you are not this lucky, try planting one.

The elder tree has been known to cure many ailments with its flowers, leaves, bark, roots, and berries. One of its most useful properties is its power to warm you in winter. If you suffer from seasonal depression, try drinking elderflower tea or wine. Pick and dry the flowers in the late spring and infuse them in boiling water to make tea. If you do not make wine, just add half a glass of wine, or a dash of whiskey, to the tea to make a hot elderflower toddy.

Elder

Every part of the elder has been used to treat illnesses and ailments,
from hiccoughs and head colds to conjunctivitis and fluid retention. It is one of the
most valuable healing plants that nature has to offer.

VERVAIN

LATIN NAME *Verbena officinalis*
OTHER NAMES *Druid's weed, holy herb, Juno's tears*
MEANING *Prophecy*

This was one of the Celts' most sacred plants and was used by the Druids of Gaul for all sorts of magical purposes. They used a vervain infusion, among other things, to wash the altar when they were preparing for sacrifices. They also used vervain for prophecy and believed that by rubbing it into their skin it was possible to achieve everything their hearts desired. In the first century A.D. the Roman writer Pliny described the magic and ritual with which the Druids harvested their sacred plant: "It should be picked when the dog star rises, but when there is no sun nor moon. The earth should first be appeased with offerings of wax and honey. Make a circle around the flower with iron, and then dig it up using the left hand."

To the ancient Egyptians, vervain was sacred to the mother goddess and goddess of love, Isis. It was thought to have originated from her tears. Isis' counterpart in ancient Rome was called Juno, hence its common name "Juno's tears."

In medieval Europe, vervain was used to predict the future and also to lift spells. If someone believed, for example, that their horse was ill because it had been bewitched, they would rub vervain into its skin to drive out the spell.

Vervain has been used as a plant of prophecy for thousands of years, and it has been known to refresh the mind and even to bestow prophetic dreams. If you are struggling over a difficult decision, take a piece of vervain and wrap it in a piece of black silk. Place it under your pillow at night and try to clear your mind before you go to sleep. Stop worrying about the problem, perhaps take a calming bath, and wind down. Once you are relaxed, allow yourself to drift gently to sleep. When you wake in the morning, the decision should appear far more in perspective, and you will be able to see clearly the path you need to take.

Vervain

The Romans revered vervain as a sacred flower and dedicated it to Venus, the goddess of love, because it was used to rekindle a dying passion; they also used it in love potions generally.

VIOLET

LATIN NAME *Viola odorata (sweet violet),*
Viola tricolor (wild pansy)
OTHER NAMES *Heartsease, love in idleness, herb trinity*
MEANING *Modesty, fidelity*

The violet is the plant of modesty because of the way it hides its flowers among its heart-shaped leaves. The shape of its leaves and its seductive scent link this delicate flower with love — hence many of its common names.

The ancient Persians and Greeks used violets to heal both the heart and the head. An infusion of violets in hot water helped to ease a broken heart and this remedy is still used today. You can also use violet tea — as the ancients did — to cure dizziness, especially the kind of floating light-headedness that goes with being in love.

In medieval times the wild pansy was one of the trinity of symbolic flowers — along with the rose and the lily — because of its three colors: purple, yellow, and white. Violets and wild pansies, either eaten or drunk as a tea, helped to purify the spirit. To this day, the violet still symbolizes purity and is a powerful charm against evil.

The word *pansy* comes from the French word *pensée*, meaning "thought." It is traditional to give wild pansies to a loved one to remember you by before going on a journey. The scent of sweet violets is conducive to thought or meditation, especially when focusing on purity or love.

VIOLET INFUSION

Handful of fresh wild violet leaves; 2 cups of boiling water; lint (a large enough piece to cover the affected skin); waterproof fabric such as oilskin. Cover the violet leaves in the boiling water and let it stand for a day. Strain off the green liquid, warm it, and soak the lint in it. Apply this as a poultice to the affected part, and cover it with the waterproof fabric. Change the dressing every few hours, and make a fresh infusion every two or three days.

Violet

Violet leaves have been used since 500 B.C. to cure skin cancers
and are used to this day as a gypsy remedy to purify
the body and rid it of tumors.

INDEX